AUTHENTIC CONGA RHYTHMS

by BOB EVANS

Biographic Notes 2
Definition of Musical Terms and Signs 3
Notation of Time Values 4
Time Signatures 4
Diagram of the Parts of the Hand Used In Playing the Conga Drum 5
The Open Tone 6
The Closed Tone 6
A Sharp Percussive Stroke 7
Grace Notes 8
The Flam 8
Tumbao 8
The Cinquillo 8
AUTHENTIC LATIN-AMERICAN RHYTHMS FOR THE CONGA DRUM 9
1. Joropo 9
2. Paso Doblé 9
3. Tango 10
4. Beguine 10
5. Samba 11
6. Baion 12
7. Guajira 13
8. Conga 14
9. Calypso 15
10. Afro-Cuban 16
11. Afro 6/8 17
12. Ñañigo 19
13. Guaracha 21
14. Rumba 22
15. Boleros 23
16. Bolero Rumba 23
17. Spanish Bolero 24
18. Merengé 25
19. Mambo 26
20. Single Mambo 27
21. Double Mambo 28
22. Cha Cha Cha 29
23. Son 30
24. Montuno 31

© 1960 HENRY ADLER, INC.
© Renewed 1988 BELWIN-MILLS PUBLISHING CORP. (ASCAP)
All Rights Administered by WARNER BROS. PUBLICATIONS U.S. INC.
All Rights Reserved including Public Performance for Profit

BIOGRAPHICAL NOTES

Bob Evans became interested in and began drumming at an early age through his father, who played drums. Drumming locally until induction into the Army he then spent 3 years in Special Service playing in marching bands and the post organized dance orchestras.

After service he enrolled in the Katherine Dunham School to study ethnic dancing and there was exposed to primitive drumming, at which he decided to give all his time and interest. At the Dunham school he studied authentic tribal and folk rhythms from two of Haiti's finest drummers, Papa Augustine and Narcisse.

After a tenure of playing Haitian songs and dances and the assimilation of Cuban rhythms he was soon featured as drum soloist in a number for an all Latin-American revue at the Boston Latin Quarter. This number was eventually placed in a long running show at the New York Latin Quarter.

Having worked primarily with dancers he became associated with dancer-choreographer, Peter Gennaro. As Mr. Gennaro's solo accompanist he played for 6 years for his numerous night club and television appearances plus his classes in Jazz.

Mr. Evans was the rehearsal drummer for the Duke Ellington television show, "A Drum Is A Woman", composing all the solo conga drum sequences.

He has appeared in the following musicals in New York: "Guys & Dolls", "The Pajama Game", "Damn Yankees", and "The Music Man". In addition to theatre appearances he has also recorded with many of the famous Latin orchestras.

Mr. Evans today is considered to be one of the foremost percussion authorities on Latin-American rhythms and music, and his knowledge and understanding are very well demonstrated in this book.

DEFINITION OF MUSICAL TERMS AND SIGNS

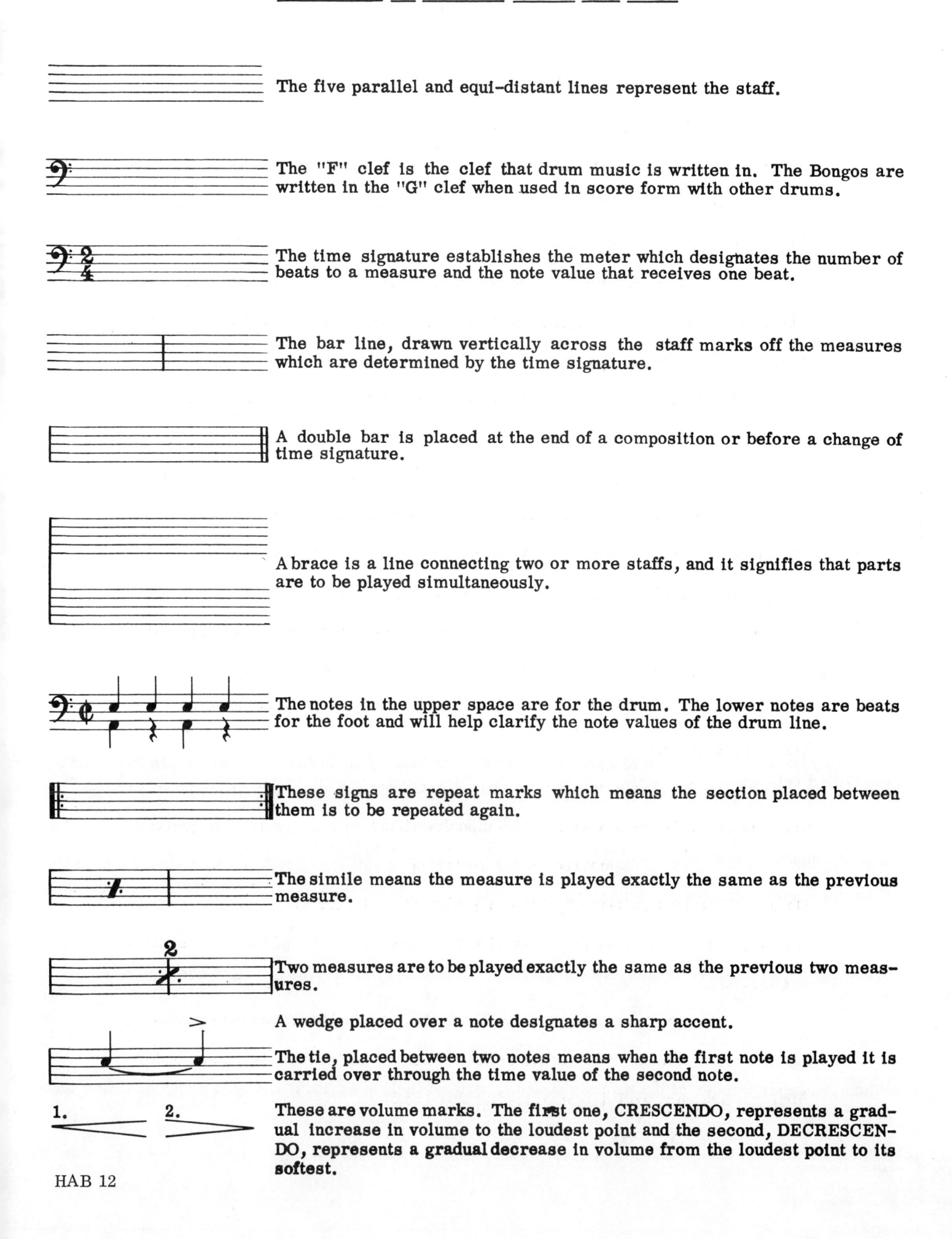

The five parallel and equi-distant lines represent the staff.

The "F" clef is the clef that drum music is written in. The Bongos are written in the "G" clef when used in score form with other drums.

The time signature establishes the meter which designates the number of beats to a measure and the note value that receives one beat.

The bar line, drawn vertically across the staff marks off the measures which are determined by the time signature.

A double bar is placed at the end of a composition or before a change of time signature.

A brace is a line connecting two or more staffs, and it signifies that parts are to be played simultaneously.

The notes in the upper space are for the drum. The lower notes are beats for the foot and will help clarify the note values of the drum line.

These signs are repeat marks which means the section placed between them is to be repeated again.

The simile means the measure is played exactly the same as the previous measure.

Two measures are to be played exactly the same as the previous two measures.

A wedge placed over a note designates a sharp accent.

The tie, placed between two notes means when the first note is played it is carried over through the time value of the second note.

These are volume marks. The first one, CRESCENDO, represents a gradual increase in volume to the loudest point and the second, DECRESCENDO, represents a gradual decrease in volume from the loudest point to its softest.

HAB 12

NOTATION OF TIME VALUES

Notes, dots and rests are the means of representing time values. The note values are:

𝆹 - Whole note   ♪ - Eighth note

𝅗𝅥 - Half note   𝅘𝅥𝅰 - Sixteenth note

♩ - Quarter note   𝅘𝅥𝅱 - Thirty-second note

The following symbols represent the corresponding rest values:

𝄻 - Whole rest   𝄾 - Eighth rest

𝄼 - Half rest   𝄿 - Sixteenth rest

𝄽 - Quarter rest   𝅀 - Thirty-second rest

A dot placed after a note is equal to half the value of the note after which it is placed:

𝆹. - Whole note and half dot (𝆹 𝅗𝅥)

𝅗𝅥. - Half note and quarter dot (𝅗𝅥 ♩)

♩. - Quarter note and eighth dot (♩ ♪)

♪. - Eighth note and sixteenth dot (♪ 𝅘𝅥𝅰)

Dots may be used after rests to increase their time values. The dotted rest values are the same as the dotted note values.

TIME SIGNATURES

C is the musical symbol for 4/4 time.

₵ is the musical symbol for 2/2 time.

Common Time

When the upper number of the time signature is written in 2, 3, or 4, it is called common time:

$$\frac{2}{4}, \frac{4}{2}, \frac{2}{4}, \frac{3}{4}, \frac{2}{8}, \frac{3}{8}, \text{ and } \frac{4}{8}.$$

Compound Time

When the upper number of the time signature is written in 6, 9, or 12, it is called compound time and the accents divide the beats into threes or triplets:

$$\frac{6}{2}, \frac{6}{4}, \frac{9}{4}, \frac{12}{4}, \frac{6}{8}, \frac{9}{8}, \frac{12}{8}, \text{ and } \frac{12}{16}.$$

DIAGRAM OF THE PARTS OF THE HAND USED IN PLAYING THE CONGA DRUM

Since the hand is the means used to produce the drum's sounds an understanding of the parts of the hand to be used is necessary since they produce the different types of beats and determine the difference in pitch. Later on the interpretation is left to the discretion of the drummer, but the different ways of achieving the desired effect must be understood by dividing the hand in sections and naming them.

FIGURE I divides the hand into the sections used for playing:

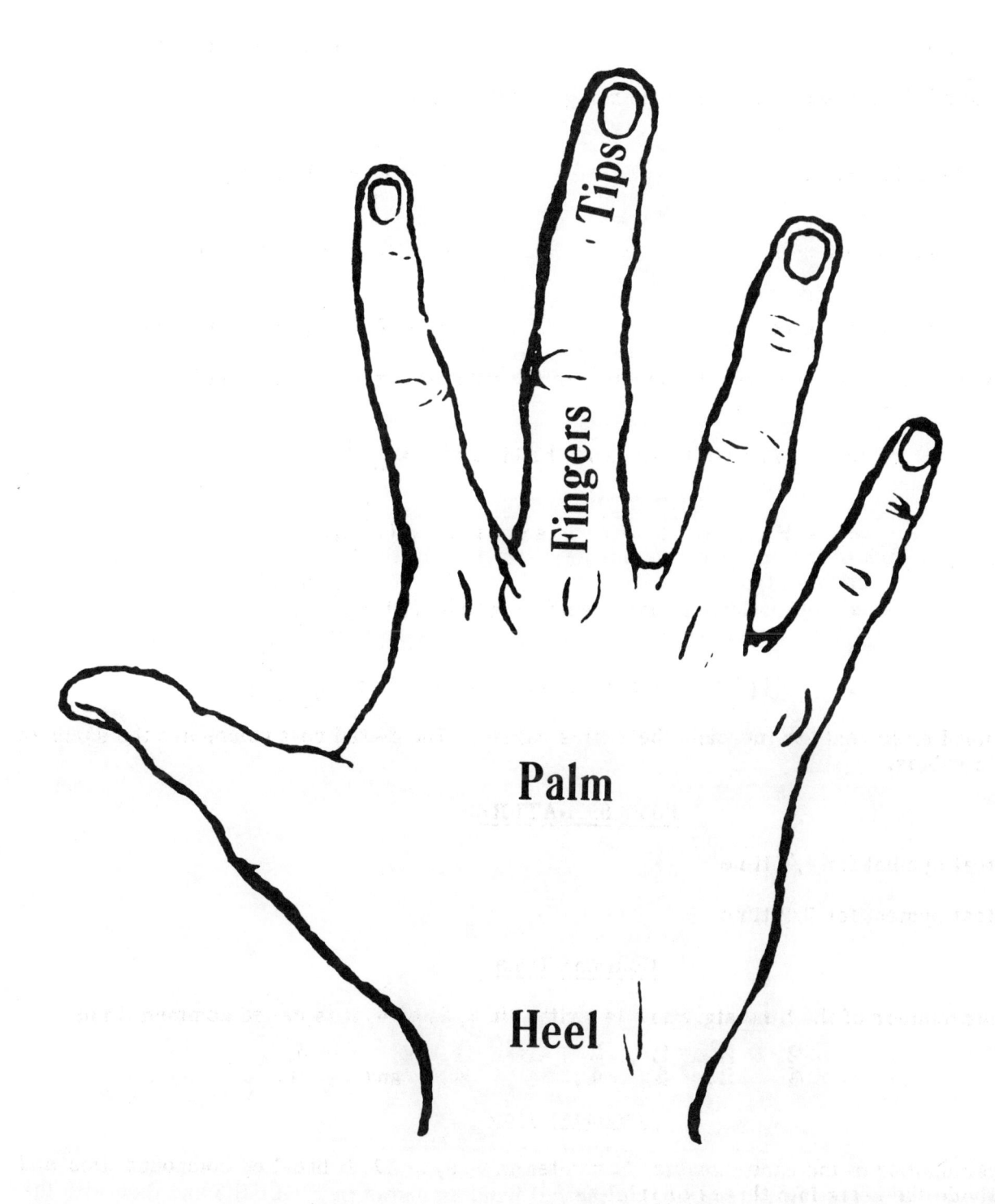

When these terms are used it means only the part of the hand designated touches the drum while the other sections are held off as not to distort the desired tone. Naturally the palm of the hand includes the heel, but not the fingers and the heel does not include either the palm of the hand or the fingers.

HAB 12

THE OPEN TONE

The first and most important tone to be achieved is the drum's true or open tone which is produced by hitting the edge of the drum with the palm of the hand, allowing the fingers to bounce off the head thus producing the open tone. Do not allow the fingers to remain on the head after hitting as the tone will be muffled. The fingers remain straight but without tension. The palm remains on the edge of the drum after the fingers **have rebounded off the head**. **Figure 2 shows the** position of hand after the stroke is done:

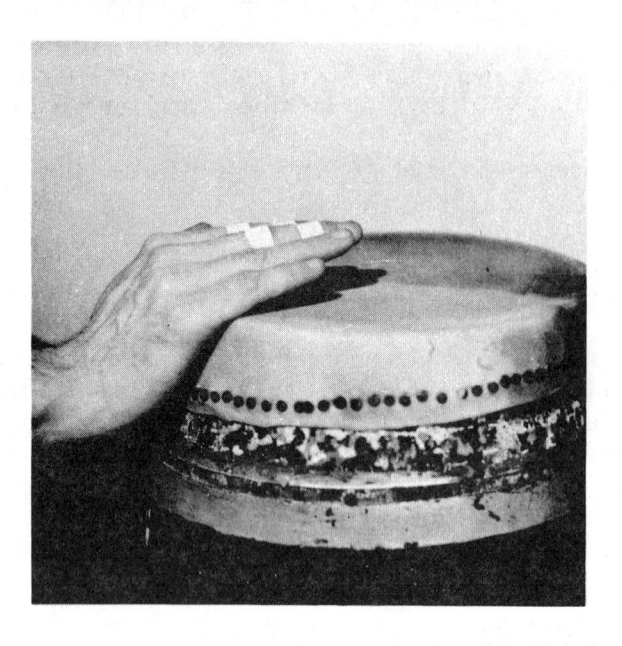

THE CLOSED TONE

The second tone, or lack of it is produced by hitting the center of the drum with either the full hand or the palm of the hand. In this stroke the palm or hand remains on the head producing a thud sound which still has resonance because of the depth and shape of the large Conga drum. This is a "no drum" stroke or closed tone. **FIGURE 3** shows the position of the hand on the drum using the full hand:

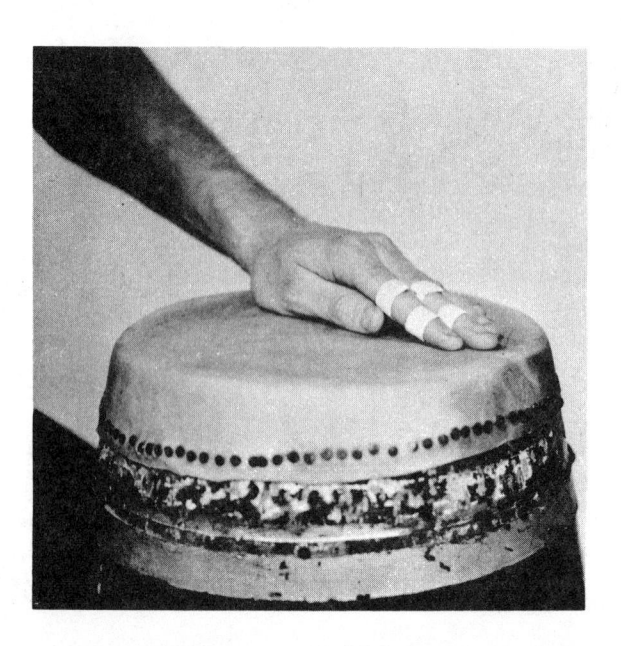

Practice striking the **center of the head using the full hand as shown in FIGURE 3** and then with the palm of the hand only. The palm is off the head in the illustration because the hand is cupped.

You will also notice that striking the head with the palm of the hand gives you a slap effect whereas the cupped hand gives more of a thud. The result you desire will determine which hand stroking you will want to use.

HAB 12

This then represents the two basic tones to be produced on a Conga drum. Other tonal effects are either modifications or extensions of the open, completely resonant tones from the edge of the drum and the closed tone of short and muffled duration produced from the center of the drum.

Over each note for the symbolic figures to represent the two tones, "O" shall stand for the Open Tone and "C" for the Closed Tone. "R" shall stand for the right hand and "L" for the left hand.

A SHARP PERCUSSIVE STROKE

There is another important sound to be gotten from the Conga drum. It can best be described as a short percussive slap, resembling at best a pistol shot, crack of a whip, or the best of descriptive similes, two pieces of wood slapped together. Of course this is giving the stroke the best of descriptions since it doesn't have the true explosive quality of any of the above effects, but nevertheless it is the loudest percussive sound the drum can produce.

The stroke is placed on the head at the edge where the open tone is done. The sound can be produced almost anywhere on the head but it is easier to get the sound nearer the edge.

The difference between the open tone sound and the slap sound is that in the open tone the fingers bounce off the head while in the slap sound they grab the head. If the palm of the hand hits a fraction ahead of the fingers it allows the fingers that small second to snap hard on the head. The hand starts the stroke with the hand straight and the snap of the fingers on the head after the palm touches the head produces the snap. FIGURE 4 shows the open hand in preparation for the stroke. FIGURE 5 shows the palm of the hand touching the edge and FIGURE 6 shows the hand position after the stroke has been executed. Notice **the fingers grasping** the head while in **the open** tone in FIGURE 3 the fingers finish the stroke off **the head:**

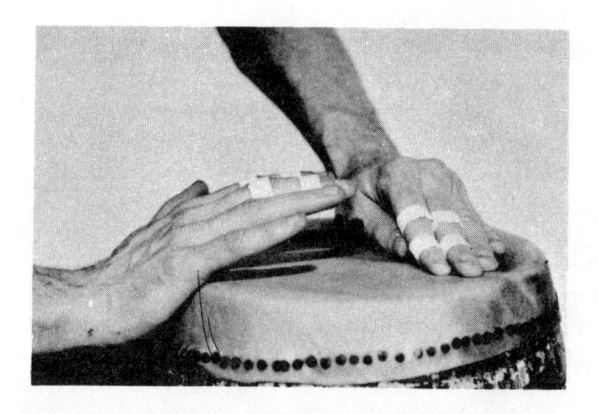

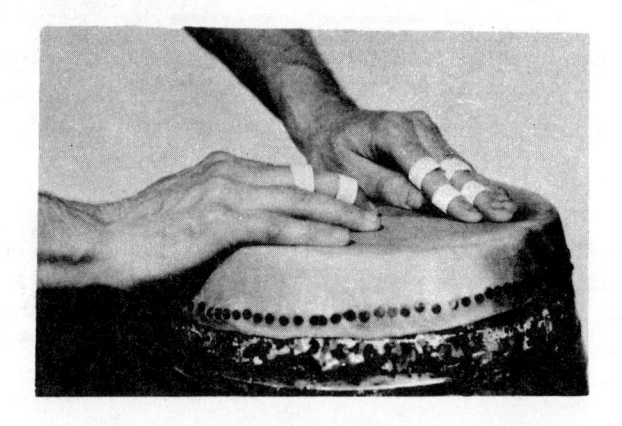

FIGURES 5 and 6 are so close as to be practically simultaneous. **The stroke will be designated by the letter "S"** in the symbols to stand for this **slap sound, in order to distinguish** it from the "O" for **the Open Tone** and the "C" for the Closed Tone.

HAB 12

GRACE NOTES

Grace notes, or appoggiaturas are smaller notes that receive no musical value but are played a fraction ahead of the adjacent note which receives the full time value. The most important and most used grace note is the Flam.

The Flam

The flam is one of the 26 rudiments used in conventional drumming. It's of great importance in hand drumming and it is used almost as much as it is in snare and field drumming. The flam consists of a light beat before the main note which is written as a grace note:

Flams can be done one handed or alternately. When practicing, the alternate stroked are better because of the hand to hand technique that's achieved even though it won't be practical all the time to execute it this way.

To start the stroke raise the right hand higher than the left and then bring them down in that position on the edge of the drum.

TUMBAO

The word Tumbao means the bass beats upon which other more complex rhythmic patterns are built. They provide the basic rhythm for other drums that take a secondary counter-rhythm. This bass beat is usually retained as a repetitious pattern throughout set rhythms and also improvisations.

THE CINQUILLO

The most important single rhythm in Latin-American music, the common denominator that binds the majority of them together is a group of five notes that have been evolved and known as a Cinquillo.

In a 2/4 meter, this is the Cinquillo figure: . This present form was derived from an early Spanish rhythmic figure that was the accompaniment used for such Spanish dances as the Habanera and the Tango. It was originally written this way: and then shortened down to just three notes: or . Eventually the original figure was lengthened to this grouping: . In 6/8 it became: and a three note version: .

In the 2/4 meter again, another measure with two beats was added to evolve into the extremely important clave rhythm: or . The clave beat, the five note Cinquillo, and its shortened three note version will all be found in great profusion in Latin-American music, especially by Cuban composers because these groupings represent the deepest emotional expressions that are to be found in Cuban music.

AUTHENTIC LATIN-AMERICAN RHYTHMS FOR THE CONGA DRUM

The rhythms in this section include those that are the most popular in the United States and the most representative of Latin-America.

The basic rhythm is given for each form plus additional variations. Some of the variations are to be used as tumbaos and also in conjunction with other percussion instruments while some variations are full enough in themselves to supply all the rhythm that is necessary. The amount of percussion needed and also what is available to you plus the special demands of a particular arrangement will determine which type of variation to use.

It is to be understood that throughout this section all repeat marks around the patterns and variations are to be interpreted as being a continuous repeat, that is, a one, two, or four measure phrase is to be repeated as long as it is desirable to do so. A one measure pattern could supply the rhythm throughout a whole number or be played only once.

On the first three rhythms shown hand drums are not played at all, but because these rhythms are so important in Latin-American music the basic rhythm of each is shown in order to become familiar with them and to show their characteristic differences from the other rhythms.

In each rhythm one example is chosen and scored with a Bongo drum part in order to show its practical use when combined with another rhythm. The choice of the two rhythms that are put together in each case is purely arbitrary since there are usually many other rhythmic possibilities that could have been used.

The Bongo drum parts will be written on the treble clef staff and the Conga drum parts in the bass clef below.

JOROPO

The Joropo is the most characteristic rhythm of Venezuela. It's in a quick tempo in either 6/8 or 3/4 with short melodic phrases and a strongly accented but simple and steady accompaniment. "Ay Trigueña" is a Joropo. A similar rhythm is the Pasillo from Colombia.

The basic rhythm is [musical notation in 3/4] which is played on a snare drum with the accent on the first beat of the measure as a roll.

PASO DOBLE

Paso Doble, meaning "double step" is a fast march in which hand drums are not used. The American Paso Doble, becoming popular in 1926 is in 3/4 meter and the Spanish Paso Doble is in 2/4. "Lady Of Spain" is an American Paso Doble and "Espana Cañi" is a Spanish Paso Doble.

Usually played on a snare drum the basic rhythms of both are in a two bar phrase. The American: [musical notation in 3/4]. The Spanish: [musical notation in 2/4]

HAB 12

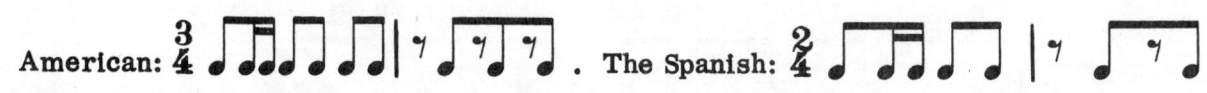

TANGO

Originated by the Moorish gypsies who called it the Milonga, the Tango was brought to Spain by them and eventually to Cuba by Negro slaves. Out of the slums of Buenos Aires it was refined and brought to the U. S. in 1914.

The Tango and the Habanera are practically identical, both having the same rhythmic figure: ♩♩ ♩ ♩ ♩. The two most important forms of Tango are the Spanish and the Argentine although there is a Brazilian Tango which is much more languid and sentimental. The Spanish Tango is in 2/4 and the Argentine Tango in 4/4 with the accent on the "and" count of four. The popular song, "It Takes Two To Tango" is in a Spanish Tango rhythm and "La Cumparsita" is in the Argentine. No hand drums are played in either Tango.

The basic Spanish Tango rhythm is: 4/8 ♩♩♩♩♩ which is played in two bar phrases on a snare drum this way: 4/8 ♩♩♩♩♩♩♩♩♩♩. The basic Argentine Tango rhythm is: 4/4 ♩ ♩ ♩ ♩♩. It would be played on a snare drum in two bar phrases with a press roll on the "and" count of four, as these two examples show:

BEGUINE

Named after the French word "bégin", meaning flirtation, the Beguine originated on the Isles of St. Lucia and Martinique.

Hand drums are used with Beguines but just to tastefully maintain the flavor. The most popular Beguine would be "Begin The Beguine".

In the basic rhythm the accent's on the "and" count of one:
The following two Conga drum patterns will furnish a fine rhythmic background for a Beguine.

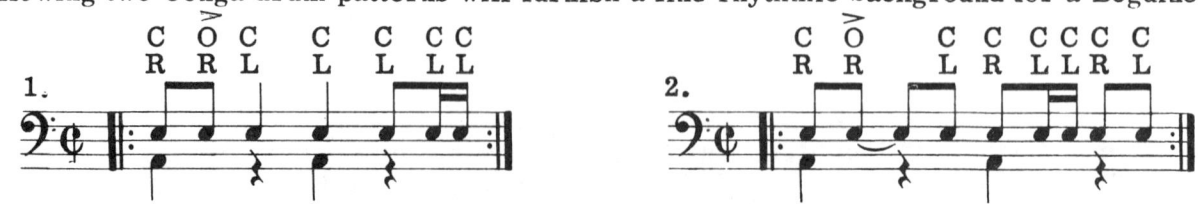

```
    C O C   C   C  C C
    R R L   L   L  L L
1.

    C O    C  C  C C C C
    R R    L  R  L L R L
2.
```

For quick reference the following symbol abbreviations will be found on every page with each new rhythm:

| R — RIGHT HAND |
| L — LEFT HAND |
| O — OPEN TONE |
| C — CLOSED TONE |
| S — SLAP TONE |

The second example is chosen to be shown with a Bongo drum part. The Bongo rhythm is unaccented to compliment the Congo drum's basic accent pattern. In the Bongo drum part the notes in the upper (E) spaces are to be played on the smaller head and the notes on the lower (C) spaces are to be played on the larger head.

```
         R RLR L R L  R L  R RLR L R L  R L
3.
Bongo

         C O    C C CCC C  C O    C C CCC C
         R R    L R LLR L  R R    L R LLR L
Conga
```

HAB 12

SAMBA

This is the national dance of Brazil and although derived from the Maxixe, it has its origin in African rhythms. A violent and fast rural type with great syncopation exists but a refined city version came to New York in 1929.

The three characteristics of the Samba are a fast tempo, 2/4 meter, and a major key. "Tico Tico" and "Brazil", which is a Samba-Cançao, are good examples of popular Samba.

Originally played on a tambourine this is the basic rhythm in a two bar phrase:

This is the basic rhythm as applied to the Conga drum:

1.

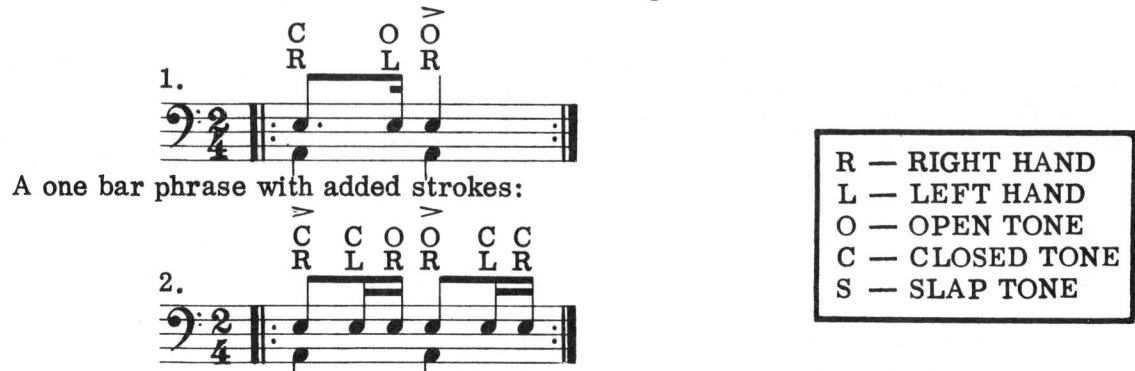

A one bar phrase with added strokes:

2.

```
R — RIGHT HAND
L — LEFT HAND
O — OPEN TONE
C — CLOSED TONE
S — SLAP TONE
```

Another one bar phrase with different stroking and tonal effect:

3.

This is identical to the example above except that it has a measure added:

4.

This is an evenly stroked rhythm for a slower Samba:

5.

A two measure Bongo pattern with the basic accents retained is added to example 3:

6.
Bongo

Conga

HAB 12

BAION

Another popular rhythm from Brazil is the Baion, a similar form to the Samba, and at times it is so alike that it's difficult to identify it as a Baion. The difference between the two is in the rhythmic pulse and general feeling. In the Baion the rhythm is more staccato while the melodic line is smoother and even flowing. In the Samba often the staccato feeling is in the melodic line while the rhythm has more of a rolling feeling. Like the Samba the Baion has its strong accent on the second beat of the measure. "Delicado" and "Anna" are Baions although other music may be played in this manner.

The basic rhythm of the Baion is the same as the basic Conga drum pattern:

This basic rhythm is applied to the Conga drum and a measure is added:

1.

R — RIGHT HAND
L — LEFT HAND
O — OPEN TONE
C — CLOSED TONE
S — SLAP TONE

By adding another 16th note the pattern achieves a fuller effect:

2.

The four 16th notes in the second measure help the rhythmic motion of the Baion:

3.

This is practically the rhythm above, but the tonal change gives it a new effect:

4.

Once more the tonal effect is changed as is the stroking and figure in the first measure:

5.

Example 3 is scored with a Bongo part that effectively reverses the pattern:

6.

Bongo

Conga

HAB 12

GUAJIRA

The rural Guajira takes its name from the Guajiros, peasants of the interior of Cuba. Related to the Punto, in its pure form it is written by alternating meters. Usually there is an eight measure intro in 6/8 meter and then the main body is either one measure of 3/4 and one measure of 6/8 or else it's a measure of 3/4 alternating with two measures of 3/8. With the two measures of 3/8 it has been called a Zarandillo, a form of Guajira. A later Guajira evolved in binary form. The first section is in 6/8 written in the minor and the second section is in 2/4, and written in the major. The last form, a city variety, is in 2/4 and resembles the Conga. This is the one using the most percussion and the one performed by orchestras.

Through all of these forms the Guajira has retained its identity by its melodic characteristics which are folksy, comparable to our "country and western" music.

The rhythm also combines well with other rhythms forming such hybrid forms as the Guajira-Son and the Guajira-Zapateo. "Junto Al Rio" and "Amor Carreteo" are typical Gaujiras.

The following Guajira rhythms for the Conga drum are the 2/4 variety. In this meter they are simple, fairly even beats. The tempo is usually Andantino Mosso.

The basic rhythm is the following from which the examples vary very little:

Two 16th notes are added to this basic phrase:

1.

R — RIGHT HAND
L — LEFT HAND
O — OPEN TONE
C — CLOSED TONE
S — SLAP TONE

Two more 16th notes added gives us a continuous pattern:

2.

Two 32nd notes are added giving 3 open tones on the last quarter note:

3.

The downbeat of each quarter note is left open for this popular one measure phrase:

4.

The basic beats of the Guajira are sustained by the Bongo drum. The second example is used for the Conga part:

5.

Bongo

Conga

HAB 12

CONGA

The Conga is the Rumba of the streets. Of Afro-Cuban origin this carnival and **parade** rhythm in march tempo was brought to the U. S. during the late 30's. As is true of the Rumba and **the** Calypso, besides drums, rhythm is often augmented by using kitchen utensils such as pots & pans, spoons, bottles, etc.

The Conga has left an indelible mark on Latin rhythms, having a distinguished strong accent on the "and" count of two in the second measure of a two measure phrase. Often this unique "push beat" will be found on the "and" count of two in the first measure instead of in the second measure.

"Para Vigo Me Voy", "Chambelona", and "Uno, Dos Y Tres" are true Congas although almost any music in 2/4 can be played with this distinctive beat.

The Conga has disappeared as a violent dance form but it has been absorbed and formalized into the Comparsa.

The basic Conga beat in 2/4 is:

With four 8th notes in the first measure this is the Conga rhythm that is used the most:

1.

| R — RIGHT HAND |
| L — LEFT HAND |
| O — OPEN TONE |
| C — CLOSED TONE |
| S — SLAP TONE |

Added 16th notes give the rhythm more pulse and drive:

2.

The first measure is syncopated and a flam is added to the accented "push beat":

3.

Triplets in the first measure with the flam "push beat":

4.

With a syncopated first measure go flams before all the strokes:

5.

The basic pattern in the Bongo drum part holds well for the syncopated rhythm of example 3:

6.

Bongo

Conga

HAB 12

CALYPSO

A rhythm from Trinidad, the characteristic beat is of African origin. Although of a simple basic rhythm Calypso is quite a free form since not only is the rhythm improvised but also the melody and lyrics, often either or both being made up on the spot. The words are satirical about topical and current events. These polysyllabic words are often rephrased completely out of meter. Cinquillo rhythms are found all through Calypso accompaniments.

In 2/4 the accent occurs on the "and" count of two. The basic rhythm is:

Applying this to the Conga drum we have:

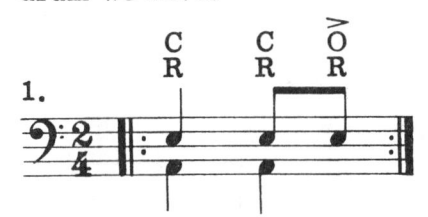

1.

```
R — RIGHT HAND
L — LEFT HAND
O — OPEN TONE
C — CLOSED TONE
S — SLAP TONE
```

Adding a 16th note to the same pattern:

2.

Syncopating the first quarter note gives a rocking beat:

3.

It is also the basic rhythm of the Spanish Tango, only with a different pulse now:

4.

The characteristic accent still remains in this 16th note example:

5.

A two measure phrase of 16th notes with an added accent in the last measure:

6.

The Bongo part is a two measure embellishing rhythm for the second example above:

7.

Bongo

Conga

HAB 12

AFRO-CUBAN

This rhythm was brought by African slaves into Cuba where it has remained unchanged except by embellishments. Unless composed specifically for a suite, Afro is not written because other slow Latin-American music in four such as the Bolero Rumba can be played in an Afro style. The basic rhythm is a one measure phrase with the distinguishing accents on "three and four". The basic rhythm:

1. With added tones for Conga drum the basic rhythm is applied this way:

2. Additional strokes fill out the rhythm:

R — RIGHT HAND
L — LEFT HAND
O — OPEN TONE
C — CLOSED TONE
S — SLAP TONE

3. A slightly different variation on the first quarter note:

4. The two 16th and an 8th notes on the first quarter re-arranged for a different figure:

5. Adding Two 16th notes to the first two quarter notes:

6. A triplet figure for the first two quarter notes but still retaining the basic accents:

7. The syncopated Bongo pattern below lends a nice contrasting rhythm to example 2:

Bongo

Conga

HAB 12

AFRO 6/8

A great many primitive rituals and religious songs and dances are done in this 6/8 meter which accounts for its prevalence in Latin-American music, even when it is used in a 2/4 meter as a contrasting counter-rhythm, i. e., when the Conga drum is in 2/4 and the Bongo & Timbale in 6/8. Improvising in 6/8 is ideal because of the nice rhythmic pulse and easier to achieve continuity this meter affords.

Basic Afro 6/8 has the accents on the "one" and "four" of the six 8th notes in the measure. This is the pulse of the 6/8:

A very basic tumbao to be used when playing with timbales, bongos and other percussion instruments is this solid foundation:

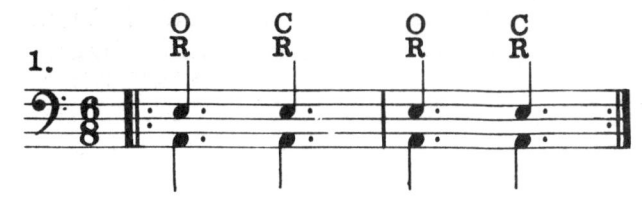

1.

R — RIGHT HAND
L — LEFT HAND
O — OPEN TONE
C — CLOSED TONE
S — SLAP TONE

A slight variation of the above rhythm is achieved by adding 8th notes and two open tones:

2.

A one measure figure with predominately open tones:

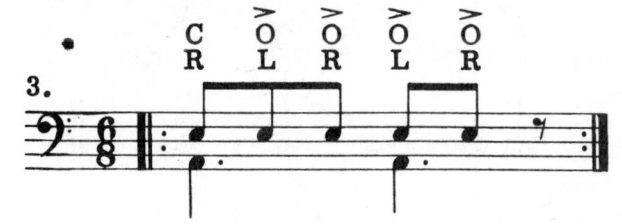

3.

A one measure figure accenting the offbeats:

4.

A two measure figure with the second beat accented by a flam:

5.

HAB 12

A two measure rhythm that stands by itself without aid from other percussion instruments:

6.

Another primitive rhythm that can be used alone:

7.

The three 16th note figures in the first two measures resemble open flams in sound and execution but the stroke starts on the beat instead of before it. They are in a metric pattern of 3/8. In the last two measures the 8th notes and rests starting after the downbeat give the effect of quarter note triplets:

8.

The following is a four measure counter-rhythm to be used against the basic beat. The flams help to bring out the irregular accenting of the short 8th note figures:

9.

Shown below is a broken rhythm of four measures for Bongos that can be used with the more even rhythm of example 6:

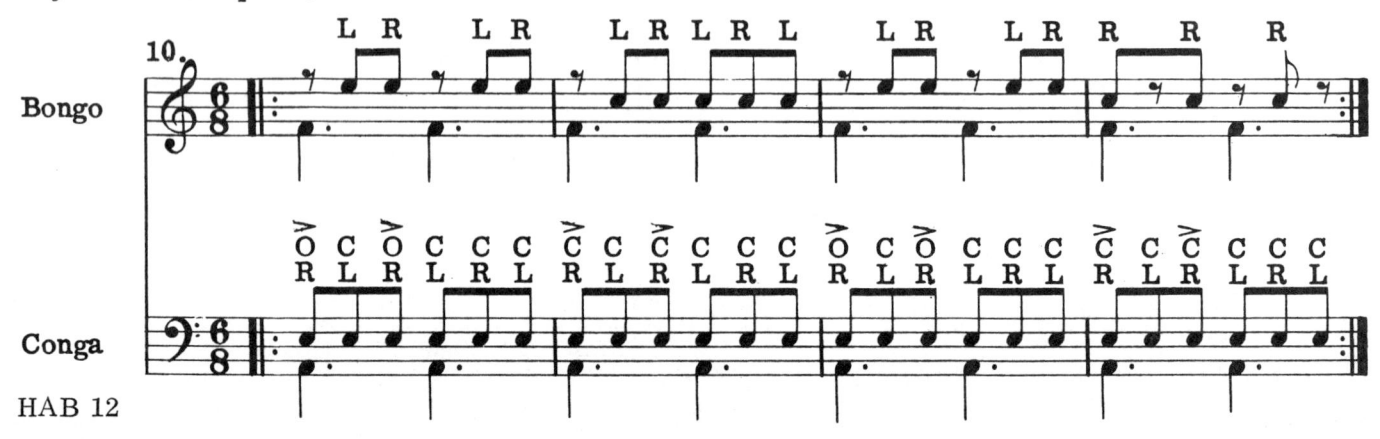

10.

Bongo

Conga

HAB 12

NAÑIGO

Nañigo is taken from a ritualistic initiation dance in Africa, the Nañiga. It is an Afro 6/8 rhythm with a distinctive rhythmic beat. A dance done at festivals and carnivals in Cuba, it is sometimes played continuously for days.

Nañigo rhythm is distinguished by a two measure phrase usually done on a cowbell. The basic Nañigo is: [musical notation in 6/8]. The measures may also be reversed in this pattern: [musical notation in 6/8]. Often Nañigo is superimposed on top of a fast 2/4 rhythm.

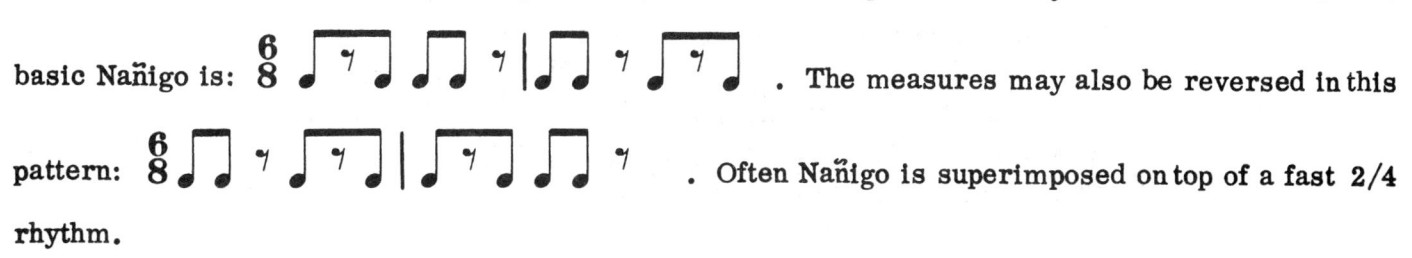

Again, as in Afro 6/8 which a Nañigo is, the Conga drum should establish a basic tumbao when other numerous percussion instruments are used.

This tumbao again applies:

1. [musical notation: O R, C R, O R, C R in 6/8]

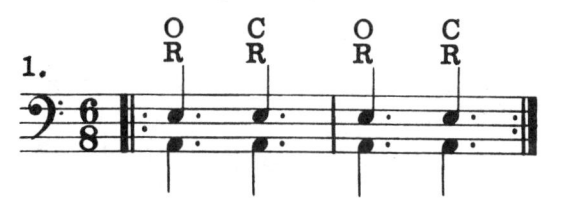

```
R — RIGHT HAND
L — LEFT HAND
O — OPEN TONE
C — CLOSED TONE
S — SLAP TONE
```

The same pulse is achieved with this figure:

2. [musical notation: O R, C L, C R, C L in 6/8]

A fuller beat to better support the Nañigo basic figure:

3. [musical notation: O R, C L, C L, O R, O L, O R, C L, C R, C L, C L in 6/8]

Another full beat and fine Conga drum support:

4. [musical notation: Ō R, C L, Ō R, C L, C R, C L, C̄ R, C L, C̄ R, C L, C R, C L in 6/8]

A broken rhythm to work not as support but as a counter-rhythm:

5. [musical notation: C L, O R, O R, C L, C R, O R, O R, C L, C R in 6/8]

A rhythm almost the reverse of the one above:

6.

The rhythm in the first two measures is in the right hand and those accents are to be played strongly. The left hand is only meant to cut the open tones short between strokes. In the last two measures the flammed quarter notes are to be stroked sharply and strongly also:

7.

In this four measure counter-rhythm the flam figures in the first measure should be executed cleanly and evenly because they start on the weak beats of the measure. The 8th notes in the last two measures are all stroked with the right hand for evenness also:

8.

The four measures of example 7 embellish the basic Nañigo beat held down by the Bongo drum part:

9.
Bongo

Conga

HAB 12

GUARACHA

The Guaracha presents a problem in trying to classify it because it has been written in so many different meters. Some have been written in 2/4, some in 3/4, and others in 6/8. Sung with guitar accompaniment the 6/8 meter has been alternated every other measure with either 3/4 or 2/4. Besides those possibilities, the melody may be anywhere from two to twelve measures in length which is repeated throughout.

The most popular form is the fast 2/4 variety which is played by dance orchestras. The Mexican Sequidilla and Jaleo are similar in this form. "La Burrita Enamorada" and "La Palmira" are in the folk forms while the popular "La Cumbanchero" is a fast 2/4 Guaracha. It has been combined with other rhythms to form hybrids such as the Guaracha-Mambo, Guaracha-Prégon, and Guaracha-Rumba. Shortened versions of the Cinquillo will be found in Guaracha accompaniments.

In the basic rhythm the beats are fairly even with the accented pulse on the last two 16th notes of the second beat:

As played by the Conga drum the rhythm is stroked in this manner:

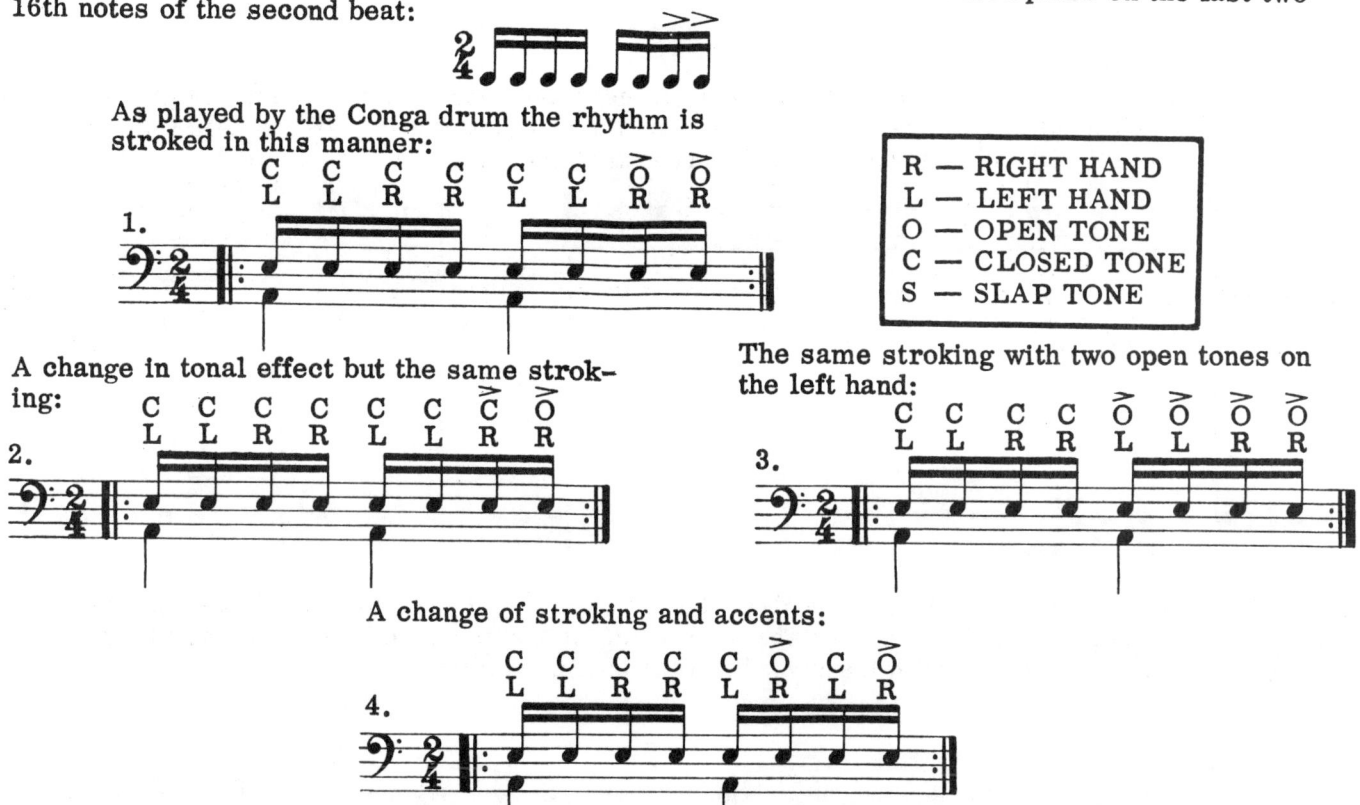

1.

| R — RIGHT HAND |
| L — LEFT HAND |
| O — OPEN TONE |
| C — CLOSED TONE |
| S — SLAP TONE |

A change in tonal effect but the same stroking:

2.

The same stroking with two open tones on the left hand:

3.

A change of stroking and accents:

4.

A repeatable four measure phrase can be made, for instance, by using the first example, the third example, the second example, and the fourth example in that order:

5.

Examples 2 and 1 in that order are used below with a one measure broken rhythmic pattern in the Bongo drum part:

6.

Bongo

Conga

HAB 12

RUMBA

The Rumba, with its roots in Africa can be traced by historical accounts as it spread from Iberia all through the West Indies and then to Cuba. That is why so many rhythms are Rumba-type such as the Calypso, Guaracha, and the Sons. Like the Guaracha it usually is taken at a very fast tempo, (but not necessarily).

Finally arriving in the U.S. in 1929, well watered down, it became an **extremely popular** dance form. In a 2/4 meter the characteristic Rumba beat is the Cinquillo figure taken by the claves for a two measure phrase:

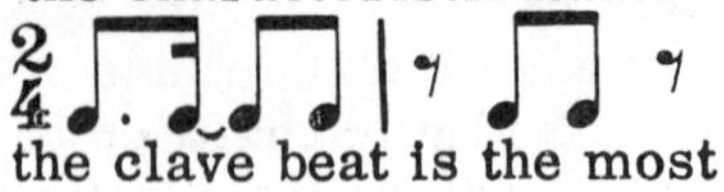

More than any other rhythm the clave beat is the most representative of a Rumba. Against this work counter-rhythms of which the simplest is a basic figure common also to Calypso: 
"Siboney" and "The Peanut Vendor" are Rumbas that are very often played very fast.

When used with other percussion this rhythm below is sufficient:

1.

| R — RIGHT HAND |
| L — LEFT HAND |
| O — OPEN TONE |
| C — CLOSED TONE |
| S — SLAP TONE |

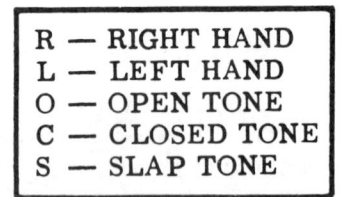

The above two measures may be added to the following two measure variation:

2.

Use this figure and stroking if the clave accents are to be played on the Conga drum:

3.

Returning again to the usual Rumba stroking this variation affords good backing:

4.

A similar variation with slightly different stress in the second measure:

5.

A smooth flowing rhythm, this time starting with the right hand which places the accents in the second measure on two unexpected weaker beats:

6.

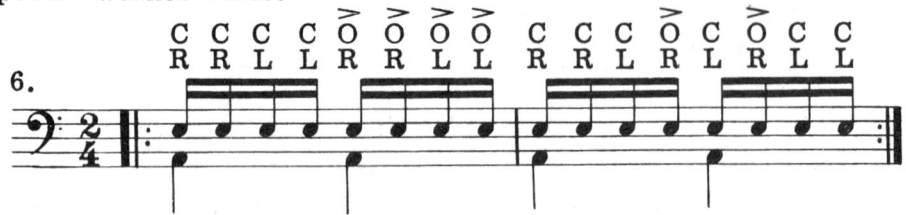

The 16th note rhythm of example 6 is off-set by a syncopated rhythm used in the Bongo part:

7.

Bongo

Conga

HAB 12

CUBAN BOLERO

The Cuban Bolero is in 2/4 meter and of moderate to slow tempo. An 8th and two 16th notes on the first quarter beat identifies the Cuban Bolero figure which was adapted from the triplet figure of the classical Spanish Bolero which is in 3/4.

The basic rhythm of the Cuban Bolero is: [2/4 notation] or the Cinquillo figure which is written this way: [2/4 notation]. The importance of the Bolero form is its use in combination with other Latin-American rhythms, such as the Bolero-Son, Bolero-Cançion, and the Bolero-Rumba.

Examples of Bolero for the Conga drum will be shown in a Bolero-Rumba rhythm since the 8th and two 16th note figure and Bolero flavor are retained in this combined form.

"Por Que Dudas" and "Las Perlas de tu Boca" are true Cuban Boleros.

BOLERO-RUMBA

The Rumba has now been relieved of its fast, driving pace, its strong accents, and its obliquely syncopated rhythms by merging with Bolero rhythms. The tempo is moderate, the meter is in a four, and although the triplet figure isn't as evident as it is in the straight Bolero, it is still suggested throughout. The pulse, dance, and feeling is still Rumba but now slower and with more elegance. "Besame Mucho" and "Siboney" are Bolero-Rumbas.

The basic rhythm is distinguishable by an 8th and two 16th notes on the first quarter:

The Conga drum may state this rhythm with this stroking:

1. C C C C C C C O C O
   L R R L R L R L R L

R — RIGHT HAND
L — LEFT HAND
O — OPEN TONE
C — CLOSED TONE
S — SLAP TONE

This pattern that repeats the first half of the measure twice may be preceded by the basic rhythm above for a two measure phrase:

2. C C C C C C C O C O   C C C C C O C C C O
   L R R L R L R L R L   L R R L R L L R R L

For a two measure phrase the basic rhythm goes first and then the same rhythm with different stroking and toal effect:

3. C C C C C C O C O   C C C C C C O O C
   L R R L R L R L R   L R R L R L R L L

The addition of an open tone on the last 8th note making three open tones consecutively:

4. C C C C C O C O   C C C C C C O O O
   L R R L R L R L   L R R L R L R L R

HAB 12

The triplet in the second measure slightly syncopates this variation:

5. [musical notation]

The two sets of 16th notes make this a good two measures to be used at the end of a four or an eight measure phrase:

6. [musical notation]

Example 4 is embellished by and also supplies the necessary downbeats for the broken rhythmic pattern of the Bongo part that is shown with it:

7. [musical notation — Bongo and Conga]

SPANISH BOLERO

The classical Spanish Bolero is not of folk origin, having been invented by a dancer in 1780. Also known under the names of Gachcha and Giatana, it is in 3/4 and usually written in the minor key in a moderate to very slow tempo.

The Cuban Bolero in 2/4 was originally derived from the Spanish Bolero and both are practically identical in tempo, mood, and feeling. Only the difference in meter and the purposes for which they are used distinguishes one from the other, as in the combining of the Cuban Bolero with the Rumba.

The characteristic figure of a Spanish Bolero is a triplet which is predominant in the music. The figure is evident in all of the following examples except for the first one:

1. [musical notation]
2. [musical notation]
3. [musical notation]
4. [musical notation]

HAB 12

MERENGUÉ

Of Spanish-Negro origin the Merengué is the national dance of the Dominican Republic, a sister island of Haiti. Possibly derived from an African dance, the Meringha, in rhythm it is very similar to the Punto.

The Spanish Merengué is usually written in the major key while the Haitian Meringué (different spelling) is usually in the minor and is sung in French.

In binary form, the first theme is 16 measures, two periods of equal length and the second theme also of 16 measures. In a moderate 2/4 meter the rhythmic pattern is a two measure phrase. The characteristic accents occur on four 16th notes on the second beat in the second measure. The accents are sometimes put in the first measure and carried over to the down beat of the next measure, but it isn't used as often as the accented second measure way is. "Mi Carino" and "La Empaliza" are good Merengués. Other 2/4 music may be adapted to the Merengué style.

This is the basic Merengué rhythm:

This is the basic rhythm reversed with the accents in the first measure now:

This basic Merengué pattern is shown with two strokings, one stroking above the other. Also the example to the right is the same rhythm as the one shown first only the measures are reversed so that the 16th note accents occur in the first measure instead, which will accustom your ear to this reverse Merengué accenting:

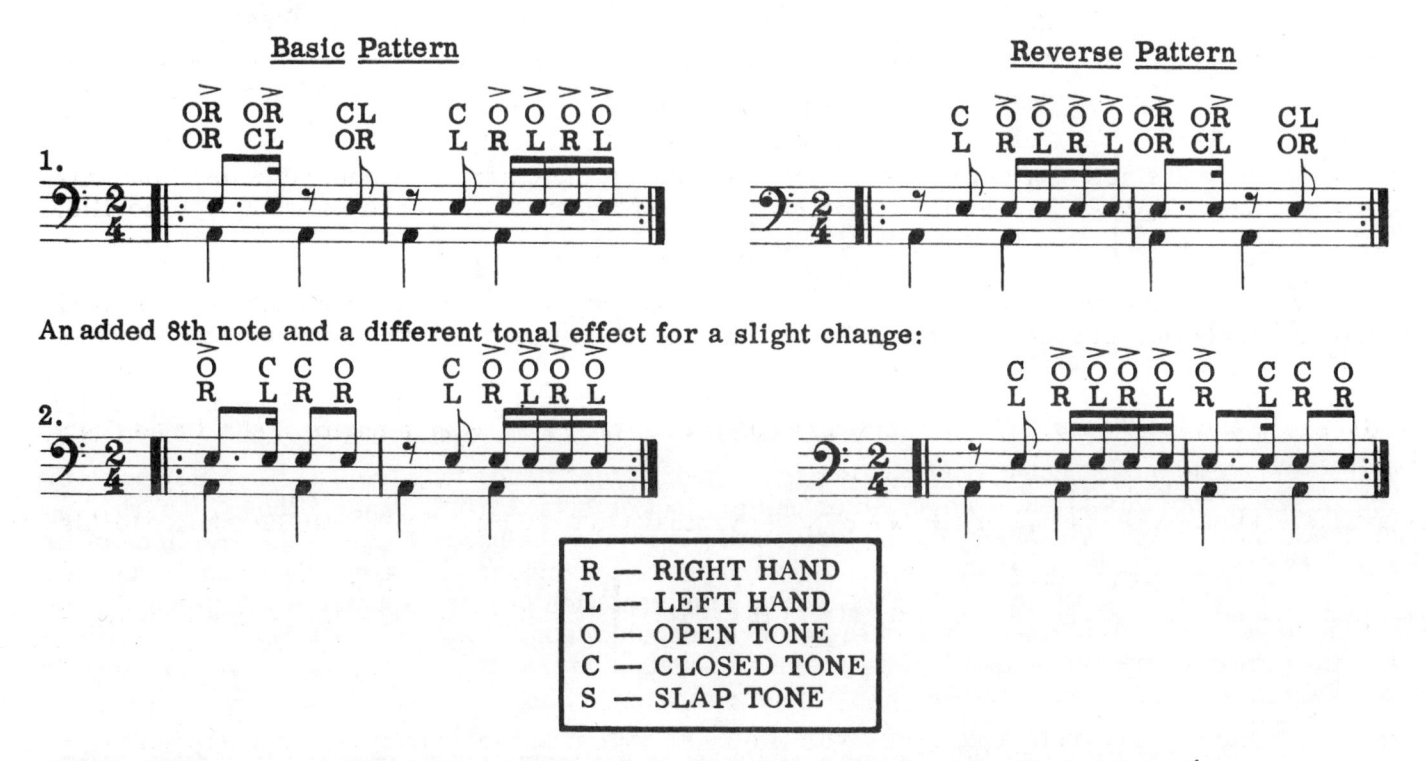

Basic Pattern   **Reverse Pattern**

An added 8th note and a different tonal effect for a slight change:

```
R — RIGHT HAND
L — LEFT HAND
O — OPEN TONE
C — CLOSED TONE
S — SLAP TONE
```

A dotted 8th rest occuring on the first beat of the first measure gives this Merengué rhythm a nice pulse:

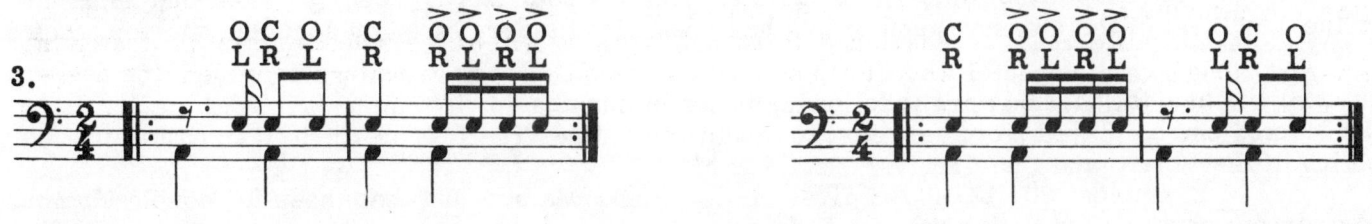

HAB 12

Basic Pattern | Reverse Pattern

With a shorter rest on the downbeat this variation has more of the continuous flow of the basic rhythm:

4.

This even flowing pattern of 8th notes can be used with a slower Merengué that also has more of an even melodic line that the faster syncopated type:

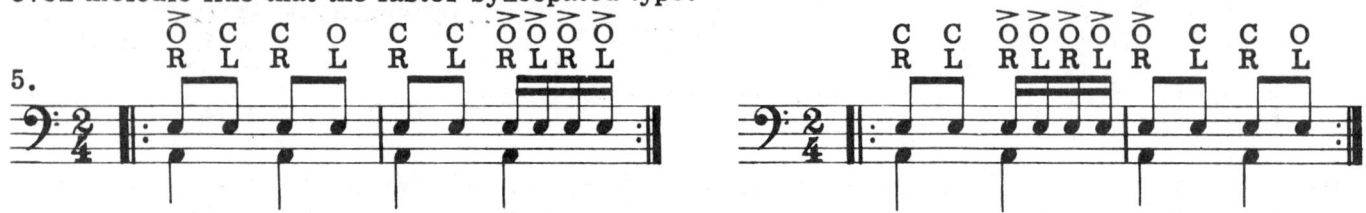

5.

The following is a variation that belongs with the fast syncopated Merengué. This particular beat helps accentuate the accented 16th notes and drives the rhythm forward:

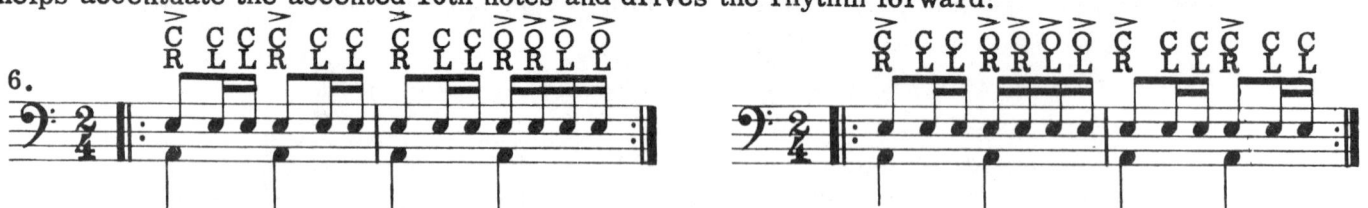

6.

Example 1, using the top stroking is shown with a Bongo rhythm that differs only in the first measure. The rhythm in the second measure of each drum states the distinguishing beat of the Merengué:

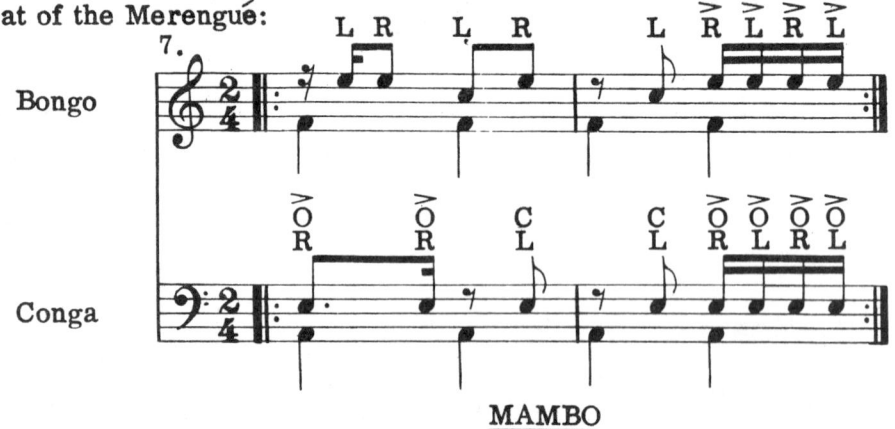

7.

Bongo

Conga

MAMBO

The most recent contribution to United States' dance fads from Latin-America is the Mambo. In a way this is as much an American product as it is Latin because although the rhythms and dance movements are Cuban, the melodies and especially the harmonies are the creations of the American Negro. Mambo is the merger of Cuban rhythms and modern contemporary jazz harmonies.

The form is not a folk form but an amalgamation of many sophisticated elements. The rhythm is derived from Rumba but with much stronger accenting, in present day interpretations. Rhythm almost dominates the melodies and is so persuasive that it has been used, unfortunately, on material that is both inferior and/or inappropriate to this rhythm, which has only succeeded in weakening the form.

Almost any music in a four may be played as a Mambo, but an excellently written and recorded example is Prez Prado's Mambo #5.

Taken from the Rumba, the basic rhythm has retained the accented "four and" 8th notes on the last beat of the measure, and to this has been added a very strongly accented quarter note on the second beat of the measure. The following is the Mambo basic rhythm:

The Mambo can be played from very fast to moderately slow. The fast or single Mambo has the four feeling of the Bolero and Cha Cha.

Examples will be shown first of the single Mambo and then those for double Mambo. Most of these rhythms can be interchanged of course because there is no set boundary so to speak between the single and double Mambo, the terms themselves often arbitrary, for the convenience of identification.

HAB 12

SINGLE MAMBO

The four rhythms below start in the first example with the basic rhythm and then develop by the addition of two 8th notes for each example. Which one to use will be determined by the type of melodic line, the tempo to be played in, and how well each can be executed at that tempo:

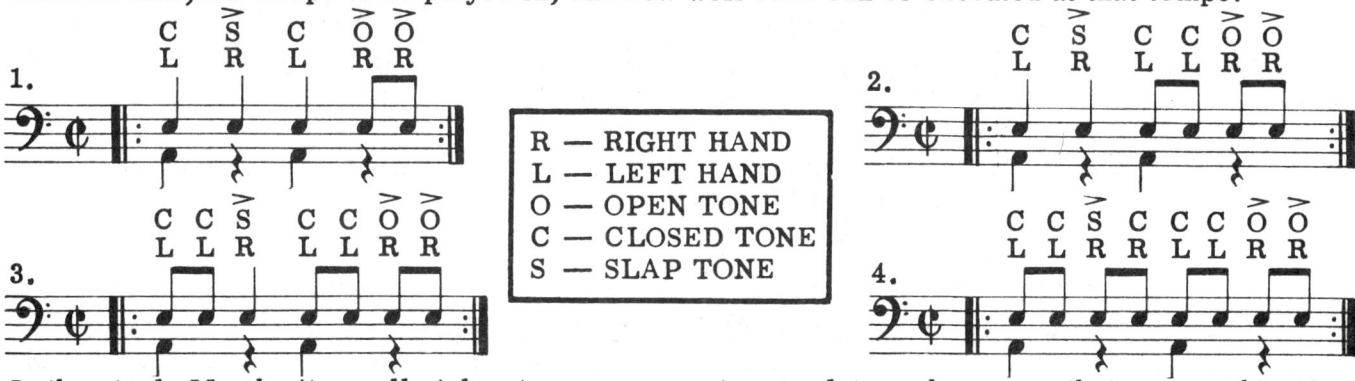

> R — RIGHT HAND
> L — LEFT HAND
> O — OPEN TONE
> C — CLOSED TONE
> S — SLAP TONE

In the single Mambo it usually takes two measures to complete a phrase, so that any combination of the four rhythms in two measure phrases is possible, and practical at times to help relieve the possibility of rhythmic monotony.

The next rhythm is a two measure phrase with a change of accents in the second measure:

The next three rhythms are four measure phrases of which the first two measures of each are the same. The accents on the second beat have been removed because they would break up the continuity and flow of the rhythms, plus the fact that it is difficult to execute them at fast tempos:

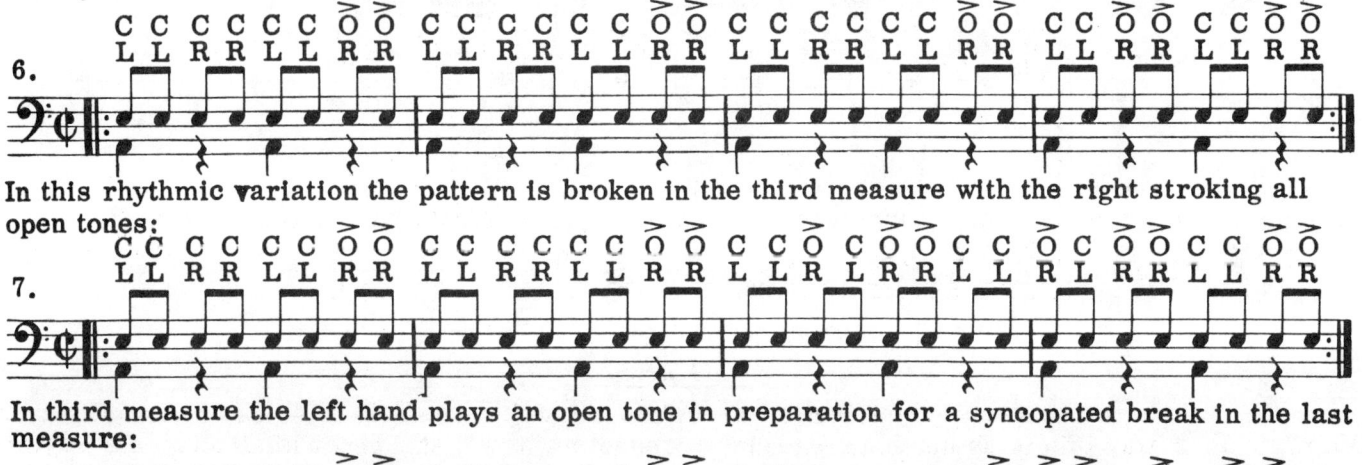

In this rhythmic variation the pattern is broken in the third measure with the right stroking all open tones:

In third measure the left hand plays an open tone in preparation for a syncopated break in the last measure:

The basic tumbao of example 3 is used to show the Conga drum's role in holding down the Mambo beat for a more intricate rhythm played against it. The highly syncopated four measures in the Bongo part needs this rock-like support or else it cannot be played correctly. It's up to the Conga drummer:

HAB 12

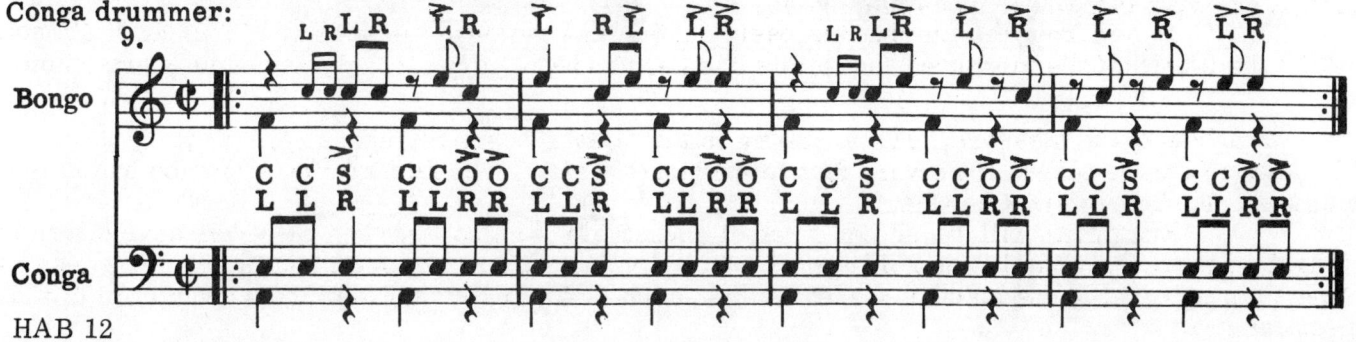

DOUBLE MAMBO

The first example is a two measure phrase in the slower four tempo with the open tones predominating:

1.

This is basically the same pattern as the one above, except that the 8th rest and added 16th notes syncopate the second measure:

2.

The next rhythm is distinguished by the subtle effect of three quarter note triplets played with a closed tone:

3.

8th note triplets this time and a tonal effect with the left hand on the closed tone and the right, accented, on the open:

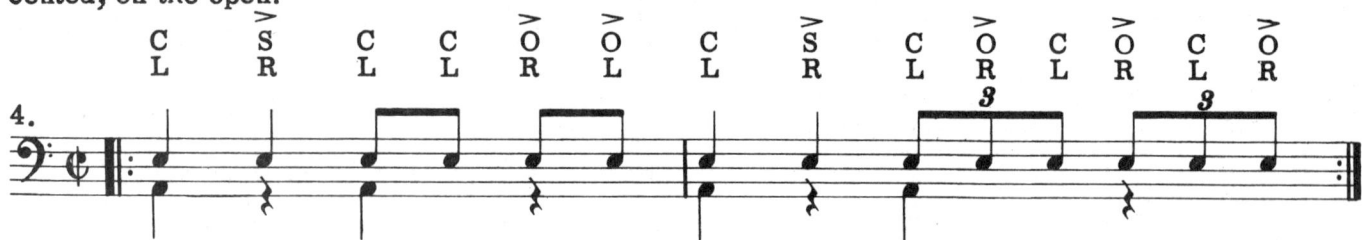

4.

Again the left hand plays the closed tones while the right hand strokes the open ones in this syncopated variation:

5.

The Mambo pattern of example 2 is used with a simple Bongo drum part. Both hands are hit simultaneously with the left and right forefingers on the fourth beat of the measure in the Bongo part:

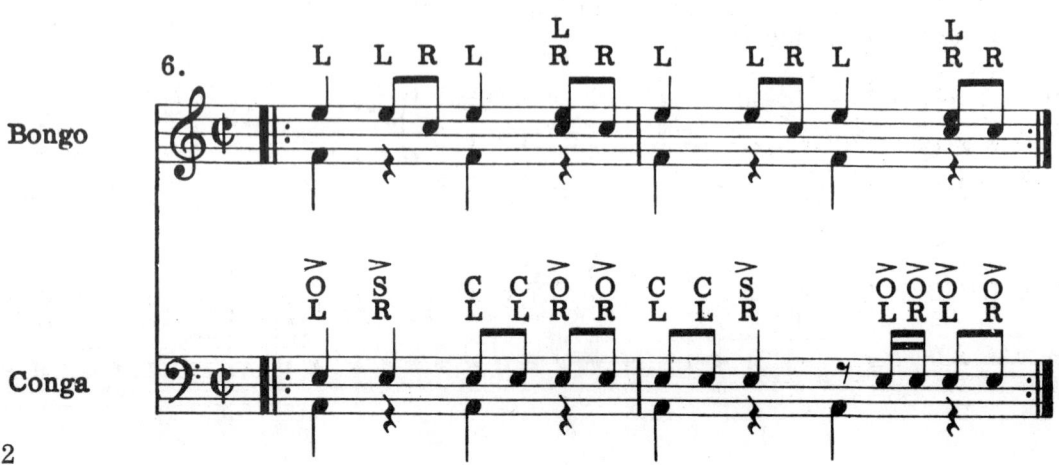

6.

Bongo

Conga

HAB 12

CHA CHA

The most recent hybrid form to evolve from the influences of the Bolero-Rumba, Double Mambo, and Jazz is the Cha Cha. In the Cha Cha the rhythmic pulse is in a very definite four, that is, that each quarter note in the measure is strongly but evenly accented. The basic rhythm for the Conga drum is still an open tone "four and" 8th note figure on the last quarter beat of the measure. As is the case with non-folk forms, any music in four can be played as a Cha Cha, but the music written putting the Cha Cha Cha (♩♩ ♩.) on the first two beats of the measure gives the right emphasis and feeling for the dancers who can choose to Cha Cha with the figure or against it.

The basic Conga drum rhythm is: ¢ ♩ ♩ ♩ ♫

The first two measure rhythm leaves an open tone on the first beat to combine with the two open 8th notes on the last quarter of the phrase:

> R — RIGHT HAND
> L — LEFT HAND
> O — OPEN TONE
> C — CLOSED TONE
> S — SLAP TONE

1.

This is a one measure rhythm that is widely used for the Cha Cha:

2.

Basically the same pattern as the first example only with the addition of two 16th note open tones:

3.

An interesting variation with open tones in the first measure and syncopated second measure:

4.

All even notes with the open tones occuring on unexpected beats:

5.

A four measure phrase with only the first and third measures being identical. The fourth measure differs in tonal effect, stroking, and note value, and can be used alone anytime as a break:

6.

The four measure example 6 with its even stroking is shown played against a syncopated two measure phrase in the Bongo part. The Bongo rhythm needs the downbeat of the Conga drum because of the 8th note rests on its downbeats:

7.
Bongo

Conga

HAB 12

SON

The Son is a Cuban development of a Spanish type folk song that came to Havana in 1916, replacing the Danzon in popularity. In a 2/4 meter it is sung in chorus with a contrasting motive for solo voice. It is made up of two sections, the first being an original refrain of not more than 8 measures and the second section, the stronger of the two being a rhythmic refrain of not more than 4 measures that are repeated over and over again, called a Montuno. Melodically simple but highly syncopated its rhythmic structure is based on a Cinquillo (♩ ♫ ♫) in which the last 8th note is split into 16ths as in the following example: ♩ ♫ ♫ ♬

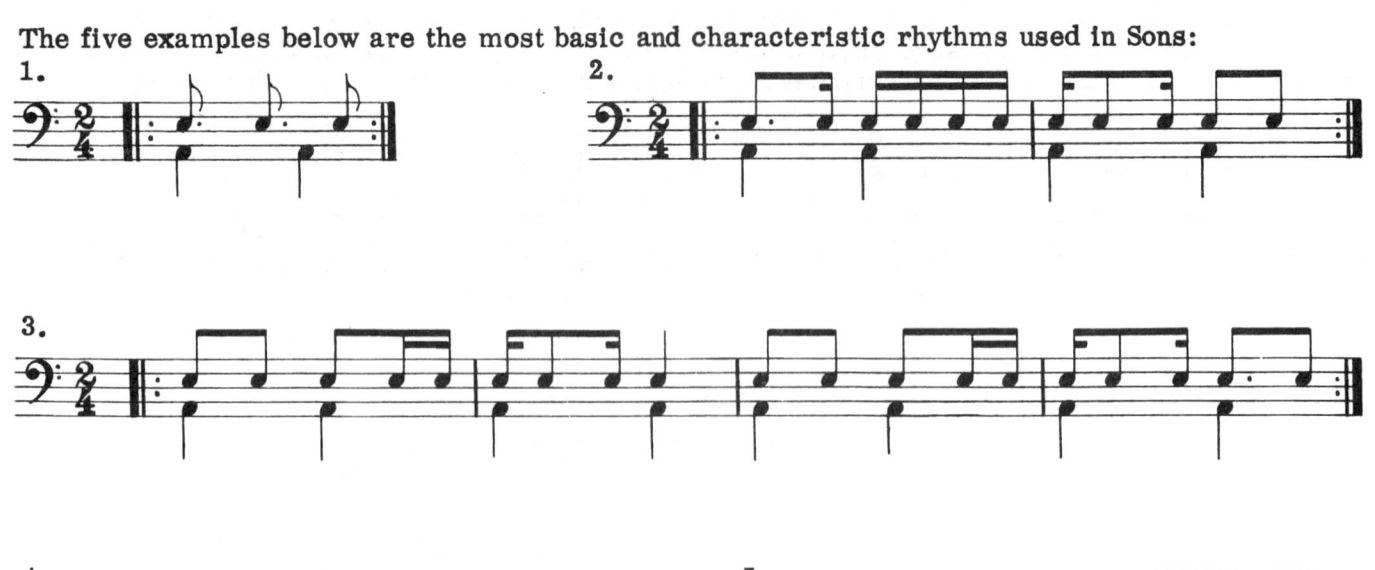

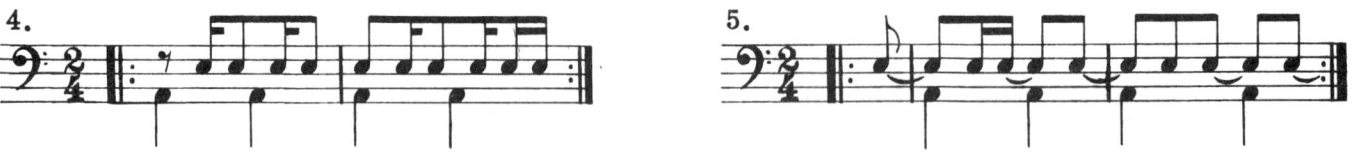

The five examples below are the most basic and characteristic rhythms used in Sons:

1.
2.
3.
4.
5.

"Sun Sun Paloma" and "La Guayabera" are pure Sons but because of the simplicity and adaptability of its melodic lines and its highly syncopated rhythms the Son has been more universally used when it is combined with other rhythms such as the Rumba, which it most resembles. Some of the hybrid forms resulting from these mergers are:

Rumba-Son - A complete synthesis of the melodies and rhythms of both.

Son-Afro Cubano - An extension of the Son with strong syncopation, it has African melodies and words. "Babalu" is a Son-Afro Cubano.

Bolero-Son - This time the rhythmic patterns come from the Bolero. Beginning in a slow tempo it speeds up halfway through to a Montuno.

Samba-Son - Rhythmically more aggressive and played with much abandon as a resurrection of its original vital form.

Son-Oriental - Less percussive and more melodically interesting since the melodies used are Spanish interpretations of oriental influences.

Tango-Son - The Spanish Habanera rhythm (♫ ♩ ♪) combines with the Son because this Tango figure is common to both forms. "Mama Ines" is a Tango-Son.

Son-Montuno - Because the Montuno is an intregal part of Son, they become an unseparable entity, one and the same thing. The Montuno, taken up next, will show the counter-rhythms and polymetrics of the Son as played in Montuno Sections.

MONTUNO

Montuno is not a rhythm but a section of a dance or song form. It is the section of the music where the melody stops and the rhythm takes over. If there is a melodic figure it is generally a melo-rhythmic phrase of two but not more than four measures repeated indefinitely. This section is also used as rhythmic support for a solo instrument improvisation. Any Cuban rhythm can have a Motnuno section. Most of them do.

The Montuno may increase or double in tempo, change in meter, or both. Of indeterminate length, it is the one section where the drummers may take turns superimposing counter-rhythms and polymetrics upon improvised rhythmic figures.

The four and eight measure counter-rhythmic phrases below are to be used in soloing as figures repeated against ensemble rhythms. They may also be used tastefully as breaks and embellishments in the other melodic sections where the rhythmic patterns are more established. Excellent for soloing is the smallest drum of the Conga drum family, the Quinto. Actually, it's a highly polished, resonant box.

Repeat marks have been eliminated because these improvisations are meant to break away from the established rhythm and they would not usually be immediately repeated again.

The first 8 measure rhythm has a very broken pattern in the first 4 measures. The strongly accented slaps are very important. The last 4 measures are in a 3/8 rhythm superimposed on the 2/4 meter:

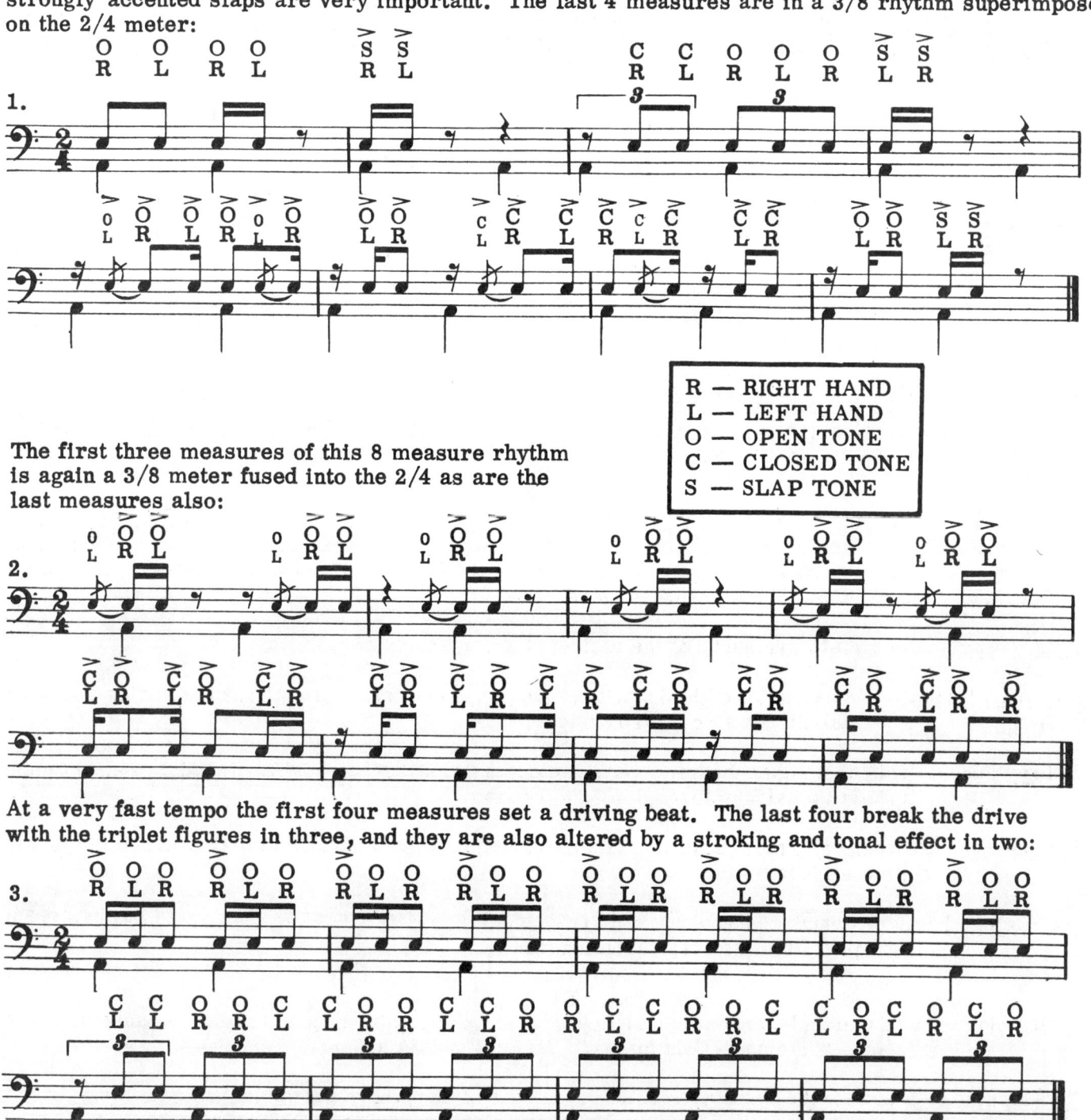

R — RIGHT HAND
L — LEFT HAND
O — OPEN TONE
C — CLOSED TONE
S — SLAP TONE

The first three measures of this 8 measure rhythm is again a 3/8 meter fused into the 2/4 as are the last measures also:

At a very fast tempo the first four measures set a driving beat. The last four break the drive with the triplet figures in three, and they are also altered by a stroking and tonal effect in two:

The meter understood in this 2/4 rhythm is 6/8 all the way through. In the last 4 measures the quarter notes fit in the 2/4 as triplets:

4.

This 8 measure counter-rhythm is in a four because it is to be taken at a moderate tempo. Measures one, three, five and seven are identical. This makes measures two, four, six, and eight, which are all different, responses to the identical measures:

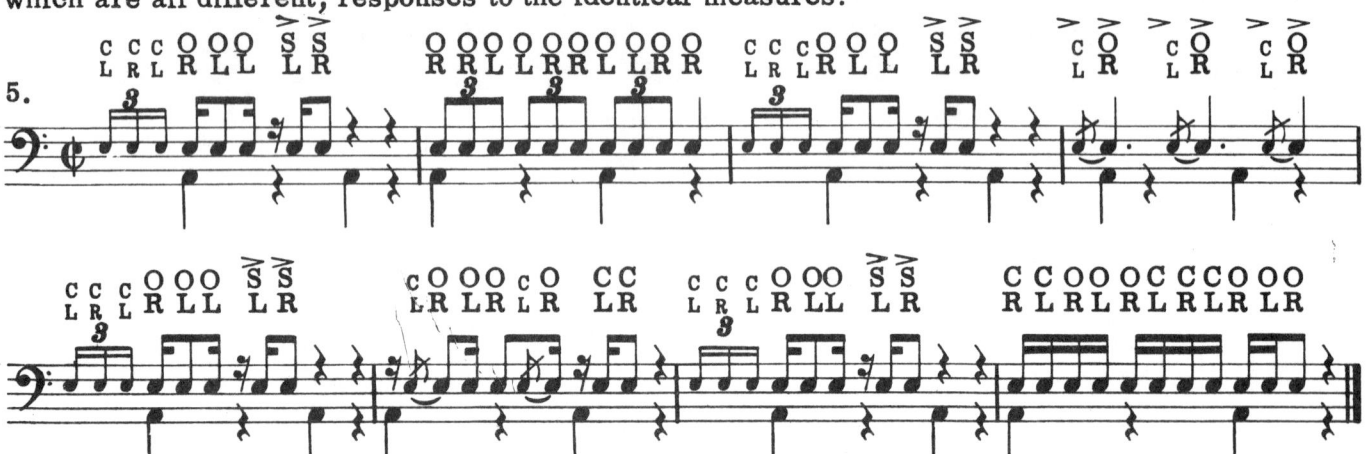

5.

Example 4 is shown with a Bongo drum rhythm. The Bongo drum drives the 2/4 rhythm strongly ahead while the Conga drum lopes along in the 6/8 feeling:

6.